This Book Belongs to

Published by Table Matters

An Imprint of Engaged Living Books

Copyright © 2022 by Jared Kent, Table Matters

ISBN 978-1-77380-222-0

All rights reserved. No part of this publication may be reproduced, stored in a retrieval system or transmitted in any form or by any means—electronic, mechanical, photocopy, recording or any other—except for brief quotations, without the prior permission of the publisher.

Table Matters books are available at a discounted rate when purchased in bulk. To place a bulk order contact us at publisher@engagedlivingbooks.com.

Printed in the United States of America

Table Matters

663 Orly Ave.

Dorval, Quebec

H9P 1G1, Canada

Visit us at tablematters.com

Conquer the Kitchen

Blank Recipe Book & Cooking Reference Guide

Jared Kent

Contents

Table of Recipes — vi
Introduction — ix

Section One: Cooking Conversions & Yields — 1

1. Measure Equivalents — 2
2. Volume Conversion (Dry and Fluid) — 2
3. Temp. Conversion — 2
4. Metric Conversion Factors — 3
5. Mass Conversion — 3
6. Length Conversion — 3

Part Two: Basic Cooking Recipes — 4

7. Basic Vinaigrette — 5
8. Quick Pickled Vegetables — 5
9. Vegetable Jelly — 5
10. Homemade Aioli — 6
11. Simple Syrup — 6
12. Vegetable Stock — 6
13. Blanched Green Vegetables — 7

Part Three: Cooking & Baking Reference Guide — 8

14. Cooking Substitutions — 9
15. Produce Seasonality — 13
16. Cooking Grains — 14
17. Moist Cooking Techniques — 14
18. Will it Freeze? — 15
19. Using Fruit and Vegetable Scraps — 16
20. Food Alkalinity Scale — 18
21. Scoville Heat Scale (Level of Spiciness) — 19
22. Which Oil to Use? — 20

23.	Blender, Food Processor or Hand Blender?	20
24.	Which Knife to Use?	21
25.	Which Pan to Use?	22
26.	What's in a Flour?	23
27.	Common Baking Ratios (by weight)	23
28.	7 Stages of Sugar Cooking	24
29.	Common Yields	25
30.	Keto-Friendly Cheat Sheet	26
31.	Common Air Fryer Times and Temperatures	27
32.	Common Instant Pot Cooking Times	28
33.	Instant Pot Cheat Sheet	29
34.	Estimated Daily Calorie Needs	30

Part Four: Cooking & Baking Tips — 31

35.	Cooking Tips	32
36.	Baking Tips	35
37.	Cooking Course	36

Section Five: Glossary of Terms — 37

38.	Glossary of Cooking Terms	38
39.	Glossary of Cookware	40
40.	Glossary of Classic Spice Blends	42

Section Six: Recipes — 45

Table of Recipes

1. _____
2. _____
3. _____
4. _____
5. _____
6. _____
7. _____
8. _____
9. _____
10. _____
11. _____
12. _____
13. _____
14. _____
15. _____
16. _____
17. _____
18. _____
19. _____
20. _____
21. _____
22. _____
23. _____
24. _____
25. _____
26. _____
27. _____
28. _____
29. _____
30. _____
31. _____
32. _____
33. _____
34. _____
35. _____
36. _____
37. _____
38. _____
39. _____
40. _____
41. _____
42. _____
43. _____
44. _____
45. _____
46. _____
47. _____
48. _____
49. _____
50. _____

51. _____
52. _____
53. _____
54. _____
55. _____
56. _____
57. _____
58. _____
59. _____
60. _____
61. _____
62. _____
63. _____
64. _____
65. _____
66. _____
67. _____
68. _____
69. _____
70. _____
71. _____
72. _____
73. _____
74. _____
75. _____

76. _____
77. _____
78. _____
79. _____
80. _____
81. _____
82. _____
83. _____
84. _____
85. _____
86. _____
87. _____
88. _____
89. _____
90. _____
91. _____
92. _____
93. _____
94. _____
95. _____
96. _____
97. _____
98. _____
99. _____
100. _____

Introduction

Recipes are one of the most intimate, heartfelt forms of communication we have as human beings. They can be passed down through generations and they can be shared between friends and total strangers alike, connecting people across time and space with the common bond of a shared meal.

When you cook someone else's recipe, or someone else cooks yours, you forge an unbreakable connection with that person. A recipe is so much more than just a set of ingredients and directions to cook a particular dish; it is a story about a time and place in your life and a blueprint to build delicious, lasting memories.

This book is a place to keep your most treasured family and personal recipes. It is filled with 100 blank recipe templates for you to write down any and every recipe you desire. Say you finally convince grandma to relinquish her top-secret recipe for that heavenly lasagna she makes. Maybe you hang around the kitchen with your grill-master father one night and scrupulously record the magic blend of herbs and spices that makes his famous barbecue sauce so delicious. Perhaps you and your partner spend several tender hours in the kitchen recreating your magical first-date dinner of the pillowy soft gnocchi from your favorite east-side trattoria.

Use this book to record those recipes and capture those cherished moments forever. Each page has ample space for you to write down the ingredients and directions for the given recipe as well as a section at the bottom of each page so you can remind yourself of the wonderful memories behind each recipe every time you cook them. You can also use that section to record any notes you may have about the recipe.

Along with the blank pages on which to record recipes, this book includes several helpful features to make your recipe keeping easier and to help improve your cooking. At the beginning of the book, there is a table of recipes so you can keep all your recipes meticulously organized and allowing you to locate your desired recipe quickly and easily.

In addition to the spaces for recipes, this book includes a treasure trove of helpful cooking tips and tools. You will find helpful charts with conversions for different measurements and temperatures so you can seamlessly switch from metric to imperial or scale your recipes up or down. There is a list of common ingredient substitutions so that your recipe is not hamstrung every time an ingredient or two is missing.

Before the blank recipe section, you will find an index of cooking and baking advice on a wide variety of topics. This is an assorted bag of tricks and bits of knowledge I have picked up over my years of professional cooking.

These topics range from technical explanations like why you should salt food from higher up, quick little recipes for basic culinary building blocks such as stock or vinaigrette, short musings on food storage and labeling, lessons I have learned about the best places to shop, and much more. These cooking tips will help you out in the kitchen and add a little spark to your cooking that will make your recipes that much more delicious.

And if you like the cooking tips, you can find many more like them by checking out our website at tablematters.com – the site has not just cooking tips but a number of delicious recipes I've made, reviews and more.

Lastly, included with the purchase of this book is a free bonus! Flip to page 33 to gain access to the online cooking course – 10 Days to Becoming a Better Cook. Over the course of 10 days, I'll teach you how to master a fundamental cooking technique while learning vegetarian recipes that are healthy, easy to make and delicious.

Now, with all of that behind you, it's time to get cooking.

Section One
Cooking Conversions & Yields

MEASURE EQUIVALENTS

1 tablespoon (tbsp)	= 3 teaspoons (tsp)
1/16 cup (c)	= 1 tablespoon (tbsp)
1/6 cup	= 2 tablespoons + 2 tsp
1/4 cup	= 4 tablespoons
1/3 cup	= 5 tablespoons + 1 tsp
3/8 cup	= 6 tablespoons
1/2 cup	= 8 tablespoons
2/3 cup	= 10 tablespoons + 2 tsp
1 cup	= 16 tbsp (or 48 tsp)
8 fluid ounces (fl oz)	= 1 cup
1 pint (pt)	= 2 cups
1 quart (qt)	= 2 pints
4 cups	= 1 quart
1 gallon (gal)	= 4 quarts
16 ounces (oz)	= 1 pound (lb)
1 milliliter (mL)	= 1 cubic centimeter (cc)
1 inch (in)	= 2.54 centimeters (cm)

VOLUME CONVERSION (Dry)

1/8 teaspoon	0.5 mL
1/4 teaspoon	1 mL
1/2 teaspoon	2 mL
3/4 teaspoon	4 mL
1 teaspoon	5 mL
1 tablespoon	15 mL
2 tablespoons	30 mL
3 tablespoons	45 mL
1/4 cup	60 mL
1/3 cup	75 mL
1/2 cup	125 mL
2/3 cup	150 mL
3/4 cup	175 mL
1 cup	250 mL
2 cups (1 pint)	500 mL
3 cups	750 mL
4 cups (1 quart)	1 L

VOLUME CONVERSION (Fluid)

1 fluid ounce (2 tbsp)	= 30 mL
4 fluid ounces (1/2 cup)	= 125 mL
8 fluid ounces (1 cup)	= 250 mL
12 fluid ounces (1.5 cups)	= 375 mL
16 fluid ounces (2 cups)	= 500 mL

TEMP. CONVERSION (Oven)

250 F	= 120 C
300 F	= 150 C
350 F	= 180 C
400 F	= 200 C
450 F	= 230 C

METRIC CONVERSION FACTORS (Mass and Volume)

MULTIPLY	BY	TO GET
Fluid Ounces	29.57	grams
Ounces (dry)	28.35	grams
Grams	0.0353	ounces
Grams	0.0022	pounds
Kilograms	2.21	pounds
Pounds	453.6	grams
Pounds	0.4536	kilograms
Quarts	0.946	liters
Quarts (dry)	67.2	cubic inches
Quarts (liquid)	57.7	cubic inches
Liters	1.0567	quarts
Gallons	3,785	cubic centimeters
Gallons	3.785	liters

MASS CONVERSION

1/2 ounce	= 14 g
1 ounce	= 28 g
4 ounces	= 115 g
8 ounces	= 230 g
10 ounces	= 280 g
12 ounces	= 340 g
16 ounces (1 lb)	= 450 g

LENGTH CONVERSION

1/16 inch	= 1.5 mm
1/8 inch	= 3 mm
1/4 inch	= 6 mm
1/2 inch	= 1.2 cm
3/4 inch	= 2 cm
1 inch	= 2.5 cm
1 foot	= 0.3 m

Part Two

Basic Cooking Recipes

Basic Cooking Recipes

Basic Vinaigrette

Ingredients

- 1 tablespoon Dijon mustard
- 2 teaspoons sugar
- ¼ cup vinegar
- ¾ cup olive oil
- pinch of salt and pepper

Directions

1. Whisk together the mustard, sugar, and vinegar
2. Slowly stream in the olive oil until combined
3. Season to taste

Quick Pickled Vegetables

Ingredients

- 1 pound thinly sliced vegetables
- 2 cups vinegar
- ½ cup sugar
- 1 teaspoon salt
- Other flavorings as desired

Directions

1. Bring the vinegar, sugar, salt, and other flavorings to a boil
2. Remove from heat and pour over sliced vegetables
3. Allow to cool and store in the fridge for up to 6 months

Vegetable Jelly

Ingredients

- 2 cups finely diced vegetables
- 2 tablespoons vegetable oil
- ½ cup vinegar
- ½ cup sugar
- Salt and pepper to taste

Directions

1. Lightly sauté the vegetables in the oil for 2-3 minutes
2. Add the vinegar, sugar, and a pinch of salt and pepper
3. Simmer for 15-20 minutes or until it cooks into a jelly-like consistency
4. Season to taste

Homemade Aioli

Ingredients

- 1 egg yolk
- 1 teaspoon Dijon mustard
- 2 teaspoons vinegar or lemon juice
- 1 cup vegetable oil, salt and pepper to taste

Directions

1. Whisk together the egg yolk, mustard, and vinegar
2. Slowly stream in the oil while whisking constantly
3. Continue until all the oil is incorporated
4. Season to taste

Simple Syrup

Ingredients

- 1 cup white sugar
- 1 cup water

Directions

1. Combine sugar and water in a small pot
2. Boil just until the sugar dissolves
3. Add citrus, herbs, or spices to the pot to infuse flavors

Use the syrup to add sweetness to drinks, dressings, and desserts

Vegetable Stock

Ingredients

- 1 large white onion, peeled and diced large
- 2 carrots, peeled and diced large
- 2 stalks celery, diced large
- 6 sprigs fresh thyme
- 4 cloves whole garlic
- 4-5 black peppercorns
- 1 gallon water

Directions

1. Combine all ingredients in a large pot
2. Simmer for 45-60 minutes
3. Strain

Blanched Green Vegetables

Ingredients

- 1 pound of green vegetables such as peas, broccoli, asparagus, green beans, etc.
- 1 gallon water
- 3 tablespoons salt
- Large bowl of ice water

Directions

1. Bring the water to a rolling boil in a large pot
2. Add the vegetables to the pot and boil for 2-3 minutes
3. Remove the vegetables and plunge into ice water for 2-3 minutes

Part Three

Cooking & Baking Reference Guide

Cooking Substitutions

Vinegar Substitutes

Apple cider vinegar - Equal amount of red wine vinegar, rice vinegar, or twice the lemon juice.

Balsamic vinegar - 1 tablespoon cider vinegar + ½ tablespoon honey for every tablespoon balsamic

Rice vinegar – 1 tablespoon white vinegar + ¼ tablespoon sugar for every tablespoon rice vinegar.

Dairy Substitutes

Buttermilk – 1 cup whole or 2% milk + 1 teaspoon lemon juice or white vinegar for 1 cup buttermilk

Cottage cheese – Equal amount ricotta cheese

Evaporated milk – Equal amount heavy cream

Heavy cream – ¾ cup half & half or whole milk + ¼ cup melted butter for 1 cup heavy cream

Yogurt – 1 cup sour cream or ¾ cup buttermilk for 1 cup yogurt

Herbs and Spices Substitutes

Fresh herbs – dried herbs, 1 teaspoon dried for every tablespoon fresh (basil, parsley, cilantro, etc.)

Fresh ginger – dried ginger, ¼ teaspoon dried for every teaspoon fresh

Fresh garlic – dried garlic, ¼ teaspoon dried for every teaspoon fresh

Chili powder – ½ teaspoon cayenne pepper + ½ teaspoon paprika for every teaspoon chili powder

Allspice – ½ teaspoon cinnamon + ¼ teaspoon each dried ginger and clove for every teaspoon allspice

Fruits and Vegetables Substitutes

Beets – Carrots or sweet potatoes in cooked recipes; cabbage in raw recipes

Brussels sprouts – Broccoli or asparagus

Butternut squash – Sweet potatoes or carrots in any recipe

Cauliflower – Broccoli in any recipe

Celery root – Parsnips or turnips

Eggplant – Portobello mushrooms in pizza, pastas, and casseroles; zucchini in stews, stir-fries, and soups

Fennel – Celery in raw recipes; white onions in cooked recipes

White potatoes – Cauliflower or celery root for a low-carb replacement, especially for mashed potatoes

Kiwi – Strawberry with a splash of lime juice in desserts

Pears – Apples or peaches in cooked recipes; apples in raw recipes

Pineapple – Green apples or oranges

Plums – Cherries

Healthy Cooking Substitutes

Breadcrumbs – Equal amount oats or bran cereal pulverized in a food processor

White rice – Equal amounts brown or wild rice

Butter/shortening (in baking) – Equal amount applesauce or prune puree

Butter (in cooking) – Equal amount olive or coconut oil

Heavy cream – Equal amount skim milk or unsweetened dairy-free milk

Pasta – Equal amount whole wheat pasta

Sour cream – Equal amount low-fat Greek yogurt

White or brown sugar (in baking) – Equal amount coconut sugar; ¾ cup honey for every cup of sugar (reduce liquid in recipe by 3 tablespoons); ¾ cup maple syrup for every cup of sugar (reduce liquid in recipe by 3 tablespoons); ⅔ cup agave nectar for every cup of sugar (reduce liquid in recipe by 3 tablespoons)

White or brown sugar (in cooking) – Equal amount coconut sugar; ¾ tablespoon honey or maple syrup for every tablespoon of sugar; ¾ tablespoon agave nectar for every tablespoon sugar; 1/8 teaspoon stevia for every tablespoon sugar.

Vegan Cooking Substitutes

Butter – Equal amount olive or coconut oil

Buttermilk – 1 cup dairy-free yogurt + 2 tablespoons lemon juice for every cup of buttermilk

Fish sauce – Equal amount of soy sauce or equal parts of soy sauce and miso paste whisked together

Gelatin – 1 teaspoon agar for 8 teaspoons powdered gelatin

Milk – Equal amounts oat, soy, almond, or coconut milk

Parmesan cheese – ½ cup finely ground cashews + ½ cup nutritional yeast flakes for every cup of parmesan cheese

Worcestershire sauce – 2 tablespoons soy sauce + 1 tablespoon balsamic vinegar for every tablespoon of Worcestershire sauce

Yogurt – Equal amount coconut, cashew, or other dairy-free yogurt

Baking Substitutions

Baking mix – Equal amount pancake mix

Baking powder – ½ teaspoon baking soda + 1 teaspoon cream of tartar for every teaspoon baking powder

Bread flour – Equal amount all-purpose flour

Brown sugar – 1 cup white sugar + 2 tablespoons molasses for every cup of brown sugar

Butter – Equal amount margarine, vegetable oil, shortening or coconut oil

Cake flour – 1 cup all-purpose flour + 2 tablespoons cornstarch for every cup of cake flour

Corn syrup – 1¼ cup white sugar + 1/3 cup water for every cup of corn syrup

Honey – Equal amount maple syrup, molasses, or corn syrup

Powdered sugar – 1 cup granulated sugar + 2 tablespoons corn starch, pulsed in the food processor until finely ground for every cup of powdered sugar

Vegetable oil – Equal amount margarine, butter, shortening, or coconut oil

Vegan Baking Substitutes

Butter – Equal amount coconut oil in cookies and granola; equal amount unsweetened applesauce in sweet bread and muffin recipes; equal amount avocado puree in fudge, brownies, and other desserts.

Heavy cream – Equal amount full-fat coconut cream; ⅔ cup almond or soy milk + ⅓ cup olive oil for 1 cup heavy cream

Whipped cream – 1 cup full-fat coconut cream, chilled and whipped in a mixer for 1 cup whipped cream

Whipped egg whites – 2 tablespoons liquid from a can of chickpeas (aquafaba) for 1 egg white

Whole Egg – ¼ cup vegetable oil for one egg; 1 tablespoon chia seeds + 5 tablespoons water; 2 tablespoons water + 1 tablespoon vegetable oil + 2 teaspoons baking powder; 1 tablespoon ground flaxseed + 3 tablespoons water; ¼ cup mashed banana or apple sauce

Gluten-free Flour Substitutes

For 1 Cup All-Purpose Wheat Flour, Substitute:

All-Purpose Gluten Free Flour Blend – 1 cup, medium flour with neutral flavor

Almond flour – 1 cup, may need a little extra egg/binder, heavier flour with nutty flavor

Arrowroot Starch – ⅓ cup, light flour with neutral flavor

Buckwheat Flour – 1 cup, heavy flour with earthy flavor, may need to add 1-2 minutes to baking time

Chickpea Flour – ¾ cup, heavy flour with a slight bean flavor

Rice Flour – ¾ cup, light flour with neutral flavor

Tapioca Flour – ⅓ cup, light flour with neutral flavor

Produce Seasonality

Cooking in season is one of the best ways to have healthy, delicious food. Seasonal produce is more likely to be grown locally, will have higher nutrient content, and will taste better. Here are some of the staple fruits and vegetables that grow in each season:

Summer

Fruit - Avocadoes, Blackberries, Blueberries, Cantaloupe, Cherries, Honeydew, Mangoes, Peaches, Pineapple, Plums, Raspberries, Strawberries, Tomatoes, Watermelon, Oranges

Vegetables - Bell Peppers, Corn, Cucumbers, Eggplant, Green Beans, Okra, Tomatillos, Yellow Squash, Zucchini

Fall

Fruit - Apples, Cranberries, Grapes, Kiwi, Lemons, Limes, Pears

Vegetables - Beets, Brussels sprouts, Cabbage, Carrots, Cauliflower, Celery, Kale, Mushrooms, Butternut squash, Acorn squash, Spaghetti squash, Pumpkin, Radishes, Rutabaga, Sweet potatoes, Swiss chard, Turnips

Winter

Fruit - Apples, Grapefruit, Kiwi, Lemons, Limes, Oranges, Pears

Vegetables - Carrots, Celery root, Celery, Collard greens, Kale, Leeks, Onions, Parsnips, Potatoes, Pumpkin, Swiss chard, Turnips

Spring

Fruit - Avocadoes, Bananas, Kiwi, Limes, Strawberries

Vegetables - Asparagus, Broccoli, Carrots, Collard greens, Mushrooms, Peas, Radishes, Rhubarb, Spinach, Swiss chard, Winter Squash

Cooking Grains

Barley – 4:1 Liquid to grain. Bring barley and water to a boil. Cover and simmer until liquid absorbs, 45-60 minutes. Yield: 1 cup dry makes about 3 ½ cups cooked.

Basmati/Jasmine Rice – 2:1 Liquid to grain. Bring rice and water to a boil, cover and simmer until the liquid absorbs, 20-25 minutes. Fluff with a fork before serving. Yield: 1 cup dry makes about 3 cups cooked.

Brown Rice – 2:1 Liquid to grain. Bring rice and water to a boil, cover and simmer until the liquid absorbs, about 30 minutes. Fluff with a fork before serving. Yield: 1 cup dry makes about 3 cups cooked.

Farro – 4:1 Liquid to grain. Bring the water to a boil with plenty of salt. Add farro into boiling water and boil 20-25 minutes until tender. Strain when cooked. Yield: 1 cup dry makes about 3 cups cooked.

Millet – 2.5:1 Liquid to grain. Bring millet and water to a boil. Cover and simmer until liquid absorbs, about 25-35 minutes. Yield: 1 cup dry makes about 4 cups cooked.

Quinoa – 1.5:1 Liquid to grain. Gently rinse quinoa before cooking. Bring quinoa and water to a boil, cover and simmer until the liquid absorbs, about 20 minutes. Fluff with a fork before serving. Yield: 1 cup dry makes about 3 cups cooked.

Steel Cut Oats – 3:1 Liquid to grain. Bring oats and water to a boil. Simmer uncovered for 35-40 minutes, stirring occasionally. Yield: 1 cup dry makes about 3 cups cooked.

Wheatberries – 8:1 Liquid to grain. Lightly rinse wheatberries. Bring water to a boil with plenty of salt. Add wheatberries into boiling water and boil for 40-45 minutes until tender. Strain when cooked.

Moist Cooking Techniques

Poach – 160 to 180°F (71 to 82°C). Hot liquid just below simmering, no bubbles.

Simmer – 185 to 205°F (85 to 96°C). Hot liquid with small-to medium sized bubbles, moving slowly.

Boil – 212°F (100°C) Very hot liquid with large bubbles, moving rapidly.

Steam – 212°F (100°C) Food placed in a basket or on a rack over boiling water.

Will it Freeze?

Cannot Freeze

- Celery
- Cucumbers
- Radish
- Fresh citrus
- Parsley
- Cilantro
- Lettuce (and other greens)

Can Freeze

Apples – Slice in half, store and freeze flat in a single layer in airtight bags. Lasts 4 months.

Apricots/Peaches – Slice in half, remove the pits. Store and freeze flat in a single layer in airtight bags. Lasts 4-6 months.

Avocadoes – Slice in half, remove the pits and skin. Store in airtight bags or container. Lasts 4-6 months.

Blueberries/Raspberries/Blackberries – Wash and dry. Store and freeze in airtight bags. Lasts up to 8 months.

Carrots – Peel, chop and dry. Freeze 1-2 hours in a single layer on a sheet pan, then transfer to an airtight bag or container. Lasts up to 1 year.

Corn – Cut kernels off cob. Freeze 1-2 hours in a single layer on a sheet pan, then transfer to an airtight bag or container. Lasts up to 8 months.

Fresh peas/Zucchini/Squash – Blanch/shock for 1 minute. Drain, dry and freeze 1-2 hours in a single layer on a sheet pan, then transfer to airtight bag or container. Lasts up to 8 months.

Kale/Broccoli/Cauliflower/Asparagus/Green Beans/Wax Beans – Blanch/shock for 1-2 minutes. Drain, dry and freeze 1-2 hours in a single layer on a sheet pan, then transfer to airtight bag or container. Lasts up to 1 year.

Potatoes/Sweet potatoes – Peel, chop and blanch/shock for 2-3 minutes. Dry and freeze 1-2 hours in a single layer on a sheet pan, then transfer to an airtight bag or container. Lasts up to 1 year.

Red bell peppers – Chop, dry and freeze 1-2 hours in a single layer on a sheet pan, then transfer to an airtight bag or container. Lasts 3-4 months

Strawberries – Remove stems. Wash and dry. Freeze 1-2 hours in a single layer on a sheet pan, then transfer to airtight bag or container. Lasts up to 8 months.

Tomatoes – Blanch/shock for 1 minutes. Remove the skin. Dry and store in airtight bags or containers. Lasts up to 6 months.

Using Fruit and Vegetable Scraps

When cooking with whole fruits and vegetables, there is often some processing that needs to be done to get to the desired product. There are peels, leaves, skins, stems and other assorted scraps that are often discarded on the path to reaching the fleshy, delicious hearts of produce.

While it's easy to throw these scraps away, you could actually be missing out on quite a lot by doing so. In many pieces of produce, the traditionally overlooked and neglected bits can carry incredible tastes and aromas that, when utilized correctly, can be given new, delicious life.

By applying a little tender loving care to these odds and ends, you can not only fortify your cooking with delicious flavors, but also stretch your dollars and minimize food waste to make sensational new dishes out of scraps you would normally throw away. Here are some creative and tasty ways to use fruit and vegetable scraps.

Apple Cores and Peels – Steep apple cores and peels in hot water for 20 minutes then strain to make a crisp, slightly sweet apple tea.

Asparagus Woody Ends – The woody, fibrous ends of asparagus are too tough to eat but they're full of earthy asparagus flavor. Simmer the woody ends in hot water for 20 minutes to make a concentrated asparagus stock you can use in soup or risotto.

Avocado Pits – While they're too tough to eat, avocado pits are full of great nutrients. Pour hot water over an avocado pit to make a light avocado tea. The pits may be a little bitter, so you may have to add some sweetener to it.

Banana Peels – Banana peels are full of potassium which is great for plants. After peeling a banana, soak the peels in water in a sealed jar for about a week. After that, remove the peels from the jar and pour the water over soil as a fertilizer to promote plant growth.

Beet, Turnip, and Radish Greens – Greens from root vegetables are delicious when cooked. They can be a little tough, so they may require some simmering to break down. Simply wash the greens, roughly chop them, and cook them with some onions, garlic, and stock until tender.

Broccoli Stalks – Once you cut the green florets off a crown of broccoli, save the thick stalks. They can be shredded to make a delicious broccoli slaw or cut up, simmered, and blended into a broccoli soup.

Carrot Tops – The leafy tops of carrots can be saved to be blended into a pesto or chopped up with garlic, vinegar, and olive oil to make an earthy carrot top chimichurri.

Cauliflower Leaves – The large leaves on the bottom of a head of cauliflower can be tossed with olive oil, salt, and pepper and baked around 300°F (150°C) until dry to make crispy cauliflower leaf chips.

Celery Leaves – The leaves of a celery stalk are often discarded, but they have a great celery flavor that's good for salads and garnishing dishes.

Citrus Peels – If you just need juice from lemons, limes, oranges, or grapefruit save the peels and steep in warm olive oil for 20-30 minutes to make a citrusy infused oil for dressings or marinades.

Corn Cobs – Once you cut the corn off the cob, simmer the bare cob in water for 45-60 minutes to make a sweet corn stock that's wonderful in soups, risottos, and pasta dishes.

Ginger Peels – Steep ginger peels in hot water for 20-30 minutes then strain to make a spicy, refreshing ginger tea.

Kale Stems – After tearing the leaves off a bunch of kale, save the stems and put them into a food processor with some nuts, parmesan, and olive oil and blend until smooth to make a bright kale stem pesto.

Parsley and Cilantro Stems – The stems of soft herbs like parsley and cilantro have more flavor than the leaves. For any recipe that calls for parsley or cilantro, just chop the stems up along with the leaves.

Pineapple Peels – After cutting the peels off a pineapple, you can put the peels into a large pitcher with sugar and water and let them sit for 2-3 days to make tepache, a sweet, lightly fermented Mexican pineapple beer.

Potato Peels – When peeling potatoes, save the peels, toss them with a little oil, and bake or fry until golden brown and crispy for a snack.

Shiitake Mushroom Stems – Remove the dry, fibrous stems from fresh shiitake mushrooms and simmer them in water for 30 minutes to make a woodsy mushroom broth to flavor soups, sauces, and risottos.

Squash Pulp – The fleshy pulp inside squash like pumpkins, butternut, acorn, and spaghetti squash is full of great flavor and healthy fiber. Pick the seeds out, and the pulp can be roasted and blended into soups and purees.

Squash Seeds – The seeds from squash like pumpkins, butternut, acorn, and spaghetti can be removed from the pulp and roasted with a little olive oil and salt until crispy to make a salty snack.

Sweet Potato Peels – Unless you're making a soup or puree, there's no need to peel sweet potatoes. The peels are quite tasty and loaded with healthy fiber, so if you're making fries or baked sweet potatoes, just go ahead and eat the peel.

Watermelon Rinds – Use a vegetable peeler to remove the hard, dark green outer rind of a watermelon. Under that, is a mostly white rind that you can slice away from the red flesh of the watermelon and pickle with apple cider vinegar, sugar, salt, and mustard seeds.

Food Alkalinity Scale

Eating foods with higher levels of alkalinity can promote weight loss and good health.

Acidity and alkalinity are measured on the pH scale, on a range of 0 to 14, with 0 being the most acidic and 14 being the most alkaline, (or basic). A pH of value of 7 is considered neutral.

Note that pH is measured on a logarithmic scale, which increases by a factor of 10. So, a food with a pH of 6 is ten times more acidic than one with a pH of 7, and a food with a pH of 5 is one hundred times more acidic than a pH of 6.

Acidic Foods

pH 1.5-3 – Carbonated water, club soda, energy drinks, soda, most liquors.

pH 3-4 – Goat cheese, vinegar, chocolate, processed foods, pickles, microwaved foods, wine.

pH 4-5 – Coffee, pistachios, cranberries, wheat, white bread, sports drinks, tomato sauce, peanuts, sugar.

pH 5-6 – Chickpeas, cooked beans, butter, canned fruit, lentils, white rice, beer, molasses, onions.

pH 6+ – Milk, yogurt, most grains, eggs, brown rice, oats, whole grain bread, tea, coconut, cooked spinach.

Neutral Foods

pH 7 – Tap water

Alkaline Foods

pH 8-9 – Apples, tomatoes, turnips, bell peppers, wild rice, cherries, almonds, fresh corn, olives, avocadoes, mushrooms, peaches, bananas, radishes, honeydew, millet, lemons, limes.

pH 9-10 – Olive oil, zucchini, mangoes, grapes, lettuce, peas, figs, melon, sweet potatoes, green beans, kiwi, pears, alfalfa sprouts, cayenne pepper.

pH 10+ – Brussels sprouts, cauliflower, raw spinach, broccoli, cabbage, artichokes, potatoes, celery, carrots, cucumbers, asparagus.

Scoville Heat Scale (Level of Spiciness)

Capsaicin is the chemical compound in chili peppers that makes them spicy. The amount of capsaicin, or level of spiciness, in peppers is measured on the Scoville Heat Scale, using Scoville Heat Units. (SHU) The scale runs from 0 to 15,000,000 SHU. Anything over 350,000 SHU is considered a "super pepper" and is exceptionally spicy. Every individual pepper you buy will vary slightly, but these are the ranges of the some of the most common chili peppers:

Bell Pepper – 0

Pepperoncini – 100-500

Banana Pepper – 0-500

Anaheim Pepper – 500-2,500

Poblano Pepper – 1,000-1,500

Ancho Chile – 1,000-1,500

Green Jalapeno – 2,500-8,000

Chipotle Pepper – 2,500-8,000

Red Jalapeno – 2,500-10,000

Fresno Pepper – 2,500-10,000

Hungarian (Wax) Peppers – 5,000-10,000

Serrano Pepper – 10,000-23,000

Tabasco Pepper – 30,000-50,000

Cayenne Pepper – 30,000-50,000

Thai (Bird's Eye) Chili – 50,000-100,000

Scotch Bonnet – 100,000-350,000

Habanero – 100,000-350,000

Red Habanero – 350,000-577,000

Ghost (Bhut Jolokia) Pepper – 855,000-1,041,427

Trinidad Scorpion Pepper – 1,200,000-2,000,000

Carolina Reaper – 1,400,000-2,200,00

Dragon's Breath – 2,300,000-2,500,000

Pepper X – 3,180,000

Pure Capsaicin – 15,000,000

Which Oil to Use?

Searing/Stir-Frying/Heavy Sautéing – Canola, vegetable, sunflower, grapeseed, corn or peanut oil

Light Sautéing/Sweating Vegetables/Boiling Pasta – Olive oil

Deep Frying – Canola, vegetable, corn or peanut oil

Roasting – Vegetable, canola, corn or peanut oil

Grilling/Broiling – Canola, corn or vegetable oil

Making Popcorn – Coconut or avocado oil

Cakes/Cookies/Brownies – Vegetable oil or shortening

Salad Dressings – Vegetable or olive oil

Marinades – Vegetable oil

Aioli – Vegetable or olive oil

Blender, Food Processor or Hand Blender?

There are all sorts of different appliances and tools to blend with including blenders, food processors, and hand (or stick) blenders. But depending on the recipe, some are better than others.

Aioli – Food processor

Barbecue sauce – Hand Blender

Chunkier Soups – Hand blender

Doughs, Pie Crust – Food processor

Finely Chopping Veggies – Food processor

Pesto – Food processor

Pulverizing breadcrumbs or nuts – Food processor

Salad dressing – Blender

Salsa – Food processor

Smooth Soups – Blender

Spice Pastes – Food processor

Vegetable Purees – Blender

Which Knife to Use?

Bread Knife – Serrated blade cuts soft food without crushing. Used for bread, slicing tomatoes.

Paring Knife – Good for de-seeding, peeling veggies, cutting small fruits and vegetables, cutting garnishes and other small cutting tasks.

Cheese Knife – Best for slicing soft and semi-soft cheese, can also be used for tomatoes.

Santoku Knife – Similar to a chef knife, but with a drop point tip to add precision. Best for slicing, dicing or mincing herbs and vegetables.

Chef Knife – Everyday workhorse knife. Use for chopping herbs, vegetables and other tasks.

Utility Knife – Coring fruits and vegetables, slicing sandwiches and wraps.

Which Pan to Use?

Frying Pan – Slope sides allow food to move around easily. Best for sautéing, scrambling eggs, cooking risotto and other foods that need stirred as they cooked.

Saucepan – Slightly smaller pot with one long handle. Best for simmering rice and other grains, cooking chutneys and jams, simmering smaller batches of soups and sauces.

Saucepot – Larger pot with two smaller handles. Best for boiling potatoes, boiling pasta, blanching vegetables and simmering larger batches of soups and sauces.

Sauté Pan – Versatile, workhorse pan. High, straight sides that lock in heat and steam and a wide bottom that offers more surface area. Best for searing, shallow-frying, braising, and poaching. Can also be used to steam rice and other grains.

Wok – Thin, light carbon steel that conducts heat very quickly. Deep sloping sides allow fast, easy movement of food. Best for quick, high heat dishes like vegetable stir-fries, fried rice, noodle dishes and other Asian dishes.

What's in a Flour?

Depending on what you're making, a recipe may call for all-purpose, bread, cake, pastry, or high-gluten flour. The main difference between these flours is the percentage of gluten in them, which is the protein found in wheat that provides structure and elasticity to baked goods. The higher protein content in a flour, the heartier it will be, and it will typically be used in baked goods with more structure, like bread.

Cake Flour: 6% protein

Pastry Flour: 8% protein

All-Purpose Flour: 8.5-9% protein (mix of 6 parts bread flour and 4 parts cake flour)

Bread Flour: 11% Protein

High Gluten Flour: 12-13% protein

Common Baking Ratios (by weight)

Pie crust – 3 parts flour: 1 part liquid: 2 parts fat

Biscuits – 3 parts flour: 2 parts liquid: 1 part fat

Cookie dough – 3 parts flour: 1 part sugar: 2 parts fat

Pound cake – 1 part flour: 1 part egg: 1 part sugar: 1 part fat

Pancakes – 2 parts flour: 2 parts liquid: 1 part egg: ½ part fat

Muffin – 2 parts flour: 2 parts liquid: 1 part egg: 1 part fat

Crepe – ½ part flour: 1 part liquid: 1 egg

Sponge cake – 1 part flour: 1 part egg: 1 part sugar

7 Stages of Sugar Cooking

As sugar cooks, it reaches certain temperatures that are ideal for different kinds of desserts, candies, and pastries. The best way to measure the temperature of cooking sugar is a candy thermometer, a specialty glass thermometer that gives exact readings up to very high temperatures. When cooking sugar, use extreme caution as a burn from hot sugar is among the most severe burns.

Thread

230°-234°F (110°-112°C)
The syrup spins a soft, loose, short thread. Makes a syrup, something you may drizzle over ice cream or another cold dessert.

Soft Ball

234°-240°F (112°-116°C)
The syrup forms a soft, pliable, sticky ball. Used in fudge, buttercreams, fondant, and Italian meringue.

Firm Ball

244°-248°F (118°-120°C)
The syrup forms a firm, but pliable, sticky ball. Used in caramel candy.

Hard Ball

250°-265°F (121°-129°C)
The syrup forms a hard, sticky ball. Used in nougat, toffee, marshmallows, gummies, and rock candy.

Soft Crack

270°-290°F (132°-143°C)
The syrup forms longer strands that are firm, but still a little pliable. Used in taffy, butterscotch, and candy apples.

Hard Crack

300°-310°F (149°-154°C)
The syrup forms stiff strands that are firm and brittle. Used in brittles and hard candy, such as lollipops.

Caramel

320°-338°F. (160°-170°C)

The syrup changes color, ranging from a light golden to a dark amber brown. Forms hard, brittle strands. Used in flan, caramel cages, and candied nuts.

Common Yields

Sometimes a recipe can call for 4 tablespoons of butter or:

All-purpose flour – 1 cup = 4.25 ounces = 120 grams

　　　　　　　　　1 pound = 3 ½ to 4 cups

Brown Sugar, Packed – 1 cup = 7.5 ounces = 220 grams

　　　　　　　　　　1 pound = 2 ¼ cups

Butter – 2 cups = 1 pound = 4 sticks

　　　1 cup = 8 ounces = 2 sticks = 16 tablespoons

　　　½ cup = 4 ounces = 1 stick = 8 tablespoons

　　　¼ cup = 2 ounce = ½ stick = 4 tablespoons

Chocolate Chips – 6 ounces = 170 grams = 1 cup

Cream Cheese – 8 ounces = 225 grams = 1 cup

Honey – 1 pound = 1 ⅓ cups

Powdered Sugar – 1 cup = 4.25 ounces = 120 grams

　　　　　　　　　1 pound = 3 ¾ to 4 cups

White Sugar – 1 cup = 7 ounces = 200 grams

　　　　　　　1 pound = 2 ½ cups

Keto-Friendly Cheat Sheet

Keto-Friendly Vegetables – Green beans, lettuce, celery, asparagus, avocado, green onions, cabbage, cauliflower, olives, cucumbers, zucchini, eggplant, kale, tomatoes, green peppers, red peppers, broccoli, mushrooms, fennel, radish, pumpkin.

Keto-Friendly Fruits – Strawberries, raspberries, blackberries, blueberries, cherries, lemons, limes (in small amounts).

Main Keto-Friendly Foods – Fish, eggs, full-fat dairy, cheese, nuts, seeds, butter, coconut oil, unsweetened coconut and almond milk.

Fruits to Avoid – Bananas, watermelon, apples, pears, grapes, pineapple, mangoes, oranges, fruit juices, peaches any frozen fruit, any dried fruit

Vegetables to Avoid – Potatoes, sweet potatoes, yams, turnips, parsnips, sweet corn, beets, peas, artichokes, cassava.

Other Foods to Avoid – Lentils, beans, chickpeas, quinoa, rice, bread, white flour, tortillas, oats, pasta, sorghum, barley, buckwheat, tofu, low-fat dairy products, margarine and other trans fats, processed snack food, soda, beer, liquor, breakfast cereal, cake, cookies, biscuits, sports drinks, ice cream.

Common Air Fryer Times and Temperatures

Bell Peppers – 400°F (200°C) 12-13 minutes, shake halfway through

Broccoli – 400°F (200°C) 7-8 minutes

Brussels sprouts – 350°F (180°C) 15-18 minutes

Cauliflower – 400°F (200°C) 10-12 minutes

Crispy Tofu – 400°F (200°C) 10 minutes, shake halfway through

Fried Pickles – 400°F (200°C) 14-20 minutes, flip halfway through

Fresh Fries – 380°F (200°C) 14-16 minutes, flip halfway through

Frozen French Fries – 400°F (200°C) 20-25 minutes

Frozen Onion Rings – 400°F (200°C) 10-12 minutes, flip halfway through

Green Beans – 370°F (190°c) 7-8 minutes Mushrooms: 380°F (195°C) 10-12 minutes, stir halfway through

Potato Chips – 360°F (185°C) 15-17 minutes, flip halfway through

Ravioli – 350°F (180°C) 8 minutes

Roasted Baby Potatoes – 400°F (205°C) 16-18 minutes, shake halfway through

Sweet Potato Fries – 375°F (190°C) 12-14 minutes, flip halfway through

Zucchini – 400°F (200°C) 12 minutes

Common Instant Pot Cooking Times

Vegetables

(at high pressure)

Asparagus: 1-2 minutes

Green Beans: 1-2 minutes

Broccoli: 1-2 minutes

Brussels Sprouts: 2-3 minutes

Butternut Squash: 4-6 minutes

Cabbage: 2-3 minutes

Carrots: 6-8 minutes

Cauliflower: 2-3 minutes

Whole Small Potatoes: 8-10 minutes

Grains

(with water to grain ratios)

Wild Rice: 20-25 minutes, 2:1 water to grain

White Rice: 4 minutes, 1:1 water to grain

Whole Sweet Potatoes: 12-15 minutes

Diced Sweet Potatoes: 2-4 minutes

Corn on the Cob: 3-4 minutes

Diced Potatoes: 3-4 minutes

Whole Large Potatoes: 12-15 minutes

Jasmine Rice: 4 minutes, 2:1 water to grain

Brown Rice: 22 minutes, 2.5:1 water to grain

Quinoa: 1 minute, 1.25:1 water to grain

Steel Cut Oats: 3-5 minutes, 3:1 water to grain

Quick Oats: 1-2 minutes, 2:1 water to grain

Couscous: 1-2 minutes, 2:1 water to grain

Millet: 10-12 minutes, 1.75:1 water to grain

Wheat Berries: 25-30 minutes, 3:1 water to grain

Pot Barley: 25-30 minutes, 3.5:1 water to grain

Pearl Barley: 20-22 minutes, 2.5:1 water to grain

Instant Pot Cheat Sheet

Instant Pot Cooking Conversions for Slow Cooker and Stove

Slow Cooker Time – 10 hours on low/ 5 hours on high. Instant Pot time: 30 minutes on high pressure

Slow Cooker Time – 8 hours on low/ 4 hours on high. Instant Pot time: 24 minutes on high pressure

Slow Cooker Time – 6 hours on low/ 3 hours on high. Instant Pot time: 18 minutes on high pressure

Slow Cooker Time – 4 hours on low/ 2 hours on high. Instant Pot time: 12 minutes on high pressure

Stove Cooking Time – Simmering 2 hours. Instant pot time: 40 minutes on high pressure

Stove Cooking Time – Simmering 1 ½ hours. Instant pot time: 30 minutes on high pressure

Stove Cooking Time – Simmering 1 hour. Instant pot time: 20 minutes on high pressure

Stove Cooking Time – Simmering 30 minutes. Instant pot time: 10 minutes on high pressure

Estimated Daily Calorie Needs

ESTIMATED DAILY CALORIE NEEDS - Female

Age	CALORIE RANGE	
	Sedentary	Active
2 to 3 years	1,000	1,400
4 to 8	1,200	1,800
9 to 13	1,600	2,200
14 to 18	1,800	2,400
19 to 30	2,000	2,400
31 to 50	1,800	2,200
51+	1,600	2,200

ESTIMATED DAILY CALORIE NEEDS - Male

Age	CALORIE RANGE	
	Sedentary	Active
2 to 3 years	1,000	1,400
4 to 8	1,400	2,000
9 to 13	1,800	2,600
14 to 18	2,200	3,200
19 to 30	2,400	3,000
31 to 50	2,200	3,000
51+	2,000	2,800

Part Four

Cooking & Baking Tips

Cooking Tips

Season from Higher Up

It may sound silly but seasoning from higher up above the food is a simple, easy way to make your food taste consistently better.

Hold your hand a good five or six inches over the food as you sprinkle salt, pepper, or any other spices into it.

When you season from that height, the spices get more evenly distributed over the surface area of the food, rather than getting concentrated in one spot.

This is a good way to ensure that every bite tastes the same and you don't get one spoonful that's loaded with black pepper while the next one is bland.

Ditch the Salt and Pepper Shakers

If you're still cooking with salt and pepper shakers, get rid of them. Instead, pour your salt and pepper into small bowls or containers and season directly with your hands.

To season dishes, take a hefty pinch of salt and sprinkle it into the dish, rubbing the salt between your fingers. Repeat with the pepper in about half the quantity.

Seasoning is a tactile act, get used to feeling the texture of salt and pepper in your fingers. Over time, you'll learn to season by feel. Look for coarser grinds of salt and pepper, the larger flakes are better for seasoning.

Toast Your Spices

Whether they're whole or powdered, a light toasting works magic on spices. Toasting spices brings out the oils, making them more fragrant and flavorful, which will assuredly make the final dish taste better.

For powdered spices like paprika or chili powder, heat them over medium-low heat in a small pan without oil for 2-3 minutes, stirring constantly, just until they become fragrant. Then, pour them out in a small bowl immediately, if they sit in a hot pan too long, they'll start to burn.

After the spices are toasted, you can use them as you normally would in the course of your recipe. Follow the same procedure with whole spices like cinnamon sticks and star anise, but just cook for an extra minute.

Roasting Fruit

One of the best ways to coax extra flavor out of fruit is to roast them. Roasting fruit slowly caramelizes their natural sugars, creating complexity and depth of flavor.

Spread blueberries or strawberries onto a sheet tray with parchment paper and roast at 375°F (190°C) for 10-15 minutes, just until they start to burst.

Then they can be used in salad dressings, in compotes or jams, on top of cheesecake or yogurt, on waffles or pancakes, or anywhere else you would use fresh berries.

Roasting berries is also a great way to use up berries in your fridge that may be going bad, or to draw extra flavor out of normally bland winter berries. Roasting grapes the same way works just as well.

Cutting Butternut Squash

As tasty as it is, butternut squash can be a pain to handle. The easiest way to deal with butternut squash is to separate it into two parts.

Cut the thick bulb off the end, then slice it in half. Roast the bulb flesh side down with until the flesh is soft, and you can scoop it out with a spoon. The roasted flesh is good for blending or mashing.

Then, peel the longer, skinnier neck of the squash with a vegetable peeler and you'll have a manageable piece of squash you can dice into even cubes.

For a butternut squash soup, you can blend the roasted flesh into the body of the soup and add the sauteed cubes in for texture.

Roasting Garlic

Roasted garlic is one of the most delicious and most versatile flavors in cooking. It's a cheap, easy way to add depth of flavor to soups, sauces, salad dressings, roasted vegetables, marinades and more.

Simply take a whole bulb of garlic, slice the top off and drizzle a little olive oil over it. Then, wrap the bulb of garlic tightly in foil and roast at 350°F (180°C) for 35-40 minutes until the cloves are golden brown and soft.

Remove the garlic from the oven and allow to cool before peeling the skin off. Once the skin is removed, put the roasted cloves in a container and submerge completely with olive oil. Cover the container with a tight-fitting lid and keep the roasted garlic in the fridge (NOT at room temperature) for up to two weeks. You can then use the roasted garlic and olive oil as needed in recipes.

Storing Fresh Herbs

For fresh basil, trim off the very bottom of the stems and store the stems in a jar with water. Leave the basil out at room temperature as refrigeration can blacken the leaves.

For other fresh herbs such as parsley, cilantro, chives, rosemary, or oregano, ensure the herbs are dry, then wrap them tightly with a damp paper towel. The paper towel will help keep the herbs crisp and fresh longer.

Label and Date Containers

Whether something is stored in the fridge or in the cupboard, a label is a great way to keep your ingredients organized.

Just take a piece of painter's tape and use a permanent marker to write a quick date on the outside of the container. This is a good way to know what's what and to use up ingredients before they go bad.

Lose the Glass Cutting Board

The cutting boards you use in your everyday cooking should be made of plastic or wood.

Glass cutting boards are terrible for knives, causing even the sharpest of knives to dull, or even break. A glass cutting board is good for serving and ornamental purposes only.

Keep Your Knives Sharp

Nothing makes life easier in the kitchen than having a good, sharp knife. Sharp knives cut everything quicker and more evenly and are actually safer than dull knives. Cutting with a dull knife requires you to put more pressure on the knife, making it more likely that the knife will slip and cut your hand.

To keep a knife sharp, use a sharpening stone to sharpen it every 1-3 months, depending on usage, and use a honing steel to maintain the edge once or twice a week.

Rotate Your Spices

Dried spices can keep for a very long time, but after a while, their flavor and aroma fades. Once a year, go through your spice cabinet and get rid of anything that's been there for more than a couple years.

Shop Where the Chefs Shop

Going to the grocery store is fine, but to make your cooking better, you need better ingredients and tools.

Swing by your local farmers market to get your produce. Look for a restaurant/chef store near you, where you can usually find bulk spices, oils, vinegars, and other dry goods at a low price. You can also find professional-grade equipment there at a bargain price compared to specialty cookware stores. A local Latin, Asian, or Middle Eastern market can also be a great place to shop for cheap, high-quality ingredients.

Baking Tips

Let Eggs Come to Room Temperature

Before baking, let eggs sit out on the counter for about 30 minutes. When eggs are at room temperature, they mix more uniformly with the other ingredients in the dough or batter.

Room temperature eggs also create more volume when whipped, which leads to lighter, fluffier baked goods.

Measure by Weight

When baking, use a kitchen scale to measure your wet and dry ingredients by weight rather than volume.

Weight is a much more accurate way to measure ingredients, leading to more consistent results. For example, one cup of flour could have two very different weights on different days, depending on the grind of the flour and the humidity in the kitchen. But if you measure by weight, it will always be the same amount of flour.

Measure with Metrics

Sorry, Americans. When it comes to baking, metric measurements are more precise and accurate. The best way to measure ingredients for a dessert? Set your kitchen scale to grams.

Sift Dry Ingredients Before Mixing

An often-overlooked step, sifting is an important way to keep baked goods light and airy. Before mixing flour, cornstarch, or other dry goods into a batter or dough, run all the dry ingredients through a mesh colander and gently tap the sides to sift the mixture through the holes. This will filter out any large lumps of flour and yield a smoother, lighter product.

Whip Cream Cold

Unlike eggs, cream whips up better when cold because the fat emulsifies quicker and stays emulsified quicker. For the best results when whipping cream, don't take the cream out of the fridge until right before whipping. If you have space in the fridge, it can even help to chill the bowl and the whip before whipping cream.

Toss Chocolate Chips in Flour

If you're adding chocolate chips, blueberries, caramel bits, or any other little morsel into a cupcake or any other batter, lightly toss them in a little bit of flour first and shake off any excess.

This light coating on the outside of the chocolate chips will keep them from sticking together so they're evenly dispersed.

Cooking Course: 10 Days to Becoming a Better Cook

Included with the purchase of this book is the cooking course, 10 Days to Becoming a Better Cook. Taught by Jared Kent, this course includes 10 hands-on cooking lessons each of which will highlight a fundamental cooking technique. Every day you will get a video lesson that will show you how to master that technique paired with an accompanying vegetarian recipe that's healthy, easy to make and delicious.

Some of the techniques included are making vegetable stock, stewing and making your own pickled vegetables.

From homemade veggie burgers to hearty soups and stews, the recipes are not just tasty but they're also laden with healthy proteins and starches like lentils, quinoa, beans, brown rice, and nuts. We also show you how to use these wonderful ingredients in new and exciting ways to create satisfying dishes that will leave you feeling full and keep you from falling off the healthy eating wagon.

But be clear, this is not just a list of 10 great recipes—this is a comprehensive dive into the critical building blocks of cookery. We tell you the how and the why behind common cooking practices and give you the tools to make your cooking healthier, more delicious, and more satisfying. We'll walk you through everything and help demystify things in the kitchen so you'll have a lot more fun cooking!

Not only will this course leave you with a rotation of terrific tasty and healthy meals, but it will sharpen your cooking skills and give you the framework you need to make countless more sensational meals of your own.

Every lesson is complete with ingredient substitutions and tips and tricks to help you along the way. All you have to do is sign up and you'll receive a daily email with a rundown of the day's lesson, the video instruction, and the recipe. Then, sit back and watch the video, cook a fantastic meal in a breeze, and enjoy that meal with the people you love. Easy as that!

Access the course by scanning the QR code or by going to the link below:

subscribe.tablematters.com/better-cook-course

Section Five
Glossary of Terms

Glossary of Cooking Terms

Al dente – Cooked to where food is still firm in the middle, typically used for pasta.

Baste – To coat a food with fat or another flavorful liquid during the cooking process, helps retain moisture and flavor.

Blanch – Partially cooking fruits, vegetables, or pasta in boiling water then shocking in ice water to stop the cooking process.

Braise – A combination cooking technique involving searing a food in a small amount of fat then slowly simmering in a flavorful liquid. Particularly useful for tough, fibrous foods that need gentle, moist heat.

Bruise – Gently bashing an ingredient with the back of the knife or other blunt object to release oils and flavorful aromas. Used on garlic, citrus peels, ginger, and other spices.

Caramelize – To brown the natural sugars found in a food, resulting in an appealing depth of flavor and golden-brown color.

Confit – Similar to poaching, slowly cooking a food by submerging it in warm fat such as butter or oil.

Deglaze – To pour a flavorful liquid (vinegar, wine, stock) into the bottom of a pan to remove bits stuck on the bottom of the pan, often used to build flavor in a sauce.

Flambé – Adding liquor to a hot pan and allowing the alcohol to cook off in a burst of flame.

Julienne – To cut ingredients into long, thin strips resembling matchsticks.

Leavening – Achieved with baking soda, baking powder, cornstarch, yeast, or steam – the process of adding air to doughs, batters, and other baked goods to make them lighter and fluffier.

Macerate – To soak fruit in a flavorful liquid.

Muddle – Used in cocktails, gently mashing ingredients in the bottom of a glass or pitcher to release oils and flavorful aromas. Used with herbs, peppers, and spices.

Poach – To gently cook foods in hot liquid just underneath a simmer.

Reduce – Slowly simmering a sauce or stock to thicken the liquid and concentrate the flavor.

Sauté – Quickly cooking foods in a pan over medium to medium-high heat in small amount of fat.

Sear – Quickly cooking foods in a pan over high heat to develop color and flavor on the outside.

Sift – Passing dry ingredients such as flour, sugar, or cornstarch through a fine strainer to remove lumps.

Steep – Infuse a liquid such as a syrup or ice cream base, with different flavors by allowing herbs, spices, or other flavorings to sit in a hot liquid.

Stiff Peaks – Used to describe whipped egg whites or cream when a whipped product reaches a firm state and does not fall.

Sweat – To gently cook vegetables at a medium-low heat to draw out moisture, but not brown them.

Tempering – Slowly equalizing the temperature of two ingredients in a recipe, such as slowly whisking hot cream into egg yolks in a custard base.

Glossary of Cookware

Candy Thermometer – Glass thermometer that reads up to 400°F, (200°C) particularly helpful for making brittle, toffee, fudge, praline, caramel, and other candy.

Digital Scale – The fastest, easiest, and most accurate way to measure ingredients, especially for baking. Can easily switch between ounces and grams.

Electric Kettle – A countertop metal pitcher that can boil water in 2-3 minutes. Very useful for boiling pasta, cooking rice, or making tea/coffee.

Funnels – Very helpful for quickly transferring liquids into bottles without spillage.

Honing Steel – Shaving microscopic particles off the edge of knives to straighten the blade and maintain the edge. Note that a honing steel does not actually sharpen the knife, it just maintains the edge.

Kitchen Shearers – A very sharp, heavy-duty pair of kitchen scissors. Especially useful for quickly cutting fresh herbs.

Mandoline Slicer – A rectangular plank with a super sharp blade, used to quickly and evenly slice or shred vegetables. Especially useful for slicing potato chips.

Melon Baller – A two-sided tool with different sized half circles on either end. Used to scoop spheres out of melons and other soft foods.

Micro Plane – Also known as a zester, use to grate citrus peels, garlic, ginger, or hard cheeses.

Mortar and Pestle – An ancient tool, usually made of granite. The stone bowl and stick are used to grind and crush raw ingredients. Can be used for spice pastes, pesto, crushing garlic, grinding spices, crushing nuts, and more. Draws out natural oils and creates more depth of flavor than the food processor.

Potato Ricer – Pushes boiled potatoes or other soft foods through small holes to create rice-sized particles. Helps to make potato gnocchi or fluffier mashed potatoes.

Salad Spinner – A perforated plastic basket inside a bowl with a lid. Use to quickly dry herbs and salad greens after washing.

Sieve – A small, fine mesh colander used for sifting the lumps out of flour and other dry ingredients.

Spice Grinder – A small, countertop grinder used to grind whole spices and dried peppers into powders. Can also be used to grind coffee beans. (Get two grinders, one for coffee and one for spices.)

Squeeze Bottles – Long plastic bottles with thin tips. Very helpful for storage, plating and creating designs with sauces. Try keeping a squeeze bottle of oil next to the stove to easily squirt into pans.

Whetstone – Sometimes called a sharpening stone, it's used to sharpen knives by grinding the metal into a finer edge. It usually has a coarse, medium, and fine side and must be lubricated with oil or water.

Wire Potato Masher – Used to quickly mash potatoes, make banana bread, mash guacamole, or mashing other soft ingredients.

Glossary of Classic Spice Blends

You often see recipes calling for seasoning blends such as Old Bay or Garam Masala. But what are those blends made of, where are they from and how can they be used?

Adobo Powder

Origin – Latin America/Caribbean

Ingredients – Oregano, onion, garlic, paprika, salt, pepper, coriander, orange, or lemon.

Flavor – Garlicky blend with a slightly sweet finish and a subtle spice. Can be dry or wet.

Use on – Wonderful on grilled and roasted veggies, in soups, rice and many other dishes.

Berbere

Origin – Ethiopia

Ingredients – Chile peppers, garlic, fenugreek, ginger, coriander, salt, other warm spices.

Flavor – Very spicy blend with a warm, pungent finish.

Use on – Great in simmered vegetable stews, rice, sprinkled on top of fries, popcorn or anywhere else you're looking to add spice.

Blackening Spice

Origin – New Orleans

Ingredients – Chili powder, salt, pepper, paprika, onion, garlic, cayenne, thyme.

Flavor – Smoky, spicy blend with jazzy notes from the onion and garlic.

Use on – Liberally coat vegetables with the blend and quickly cook in a very hot pan to blacken the outside. Can also be used to season gumbo, jambalaya, and other Cajun/Creole dishes.

Everything Spice

Origin – America

Ingredients – Black and white sesame seeds, salt, onion, garlic, poppy seeds

Flavor – Nutty, garlicky blend with a hint of sweetness.

Use on – Primarily used on bagels but is good on sweet potatoes, on fries, popcorn, hummus, burger buns, folded into compound butters and more.

Fines Herbs

Origin – France

Ingredients – Parsley, chives, tarragon, and chervil.

Flavor – Can be fresh or dry. A delicate blend of soft, flavorful herbs that adds fresh, herbaceous notes to food.

Use on – Used in sauces, pastas, soups, vegetable dishes and other dishes where fresh herbs are found.

Five Spice Powder

Origin – China

Ingredients – Fennel seed, cinnamon, star anise, clove, Szechuan peppercorn. Sometimes ground ginger or coriander will be added.

Flavor – Nutty, sweet blend with a tangy, numbing finish from the peppercorns.

Use on – Used to season noodle and rice dishes, dumplings, roast vegetables, and more. Try candied nuts with five spice powder, pairs particularly well with spicy dishes.

Garam Masala

Origin – India

Ingredients – Cinnamon, mace, coriander, fennel seeds, cardamom, cumin, peppercorns, cloves, bay leaves.

Flavor – Complex blend with a warm, earthy flavor and a very gentle spice.

Use on – Widely used in many Indian dishes from curries to salad dressings, oftentimes complements spicier ingredients.

Herbs de Provence

Origin – Southern France

Ingredients – Thyme, basil, rosemary, tarragon, marjoram, savory, oregano, and bay leaf.

Flavor – Vibrant blend of hearty, aromatic herbs.

Use on – Widely used across many different French and Mediterranean dishes.

Italian Seasoning

Origin – Italy

Ingredients – Basil, thyme, oregano, garlic.

Flavor – Can be fresh or dried. Sweet and savory blend that imparts classic Italian flavor.

Use on – pasta sauces, pizza, bread and other Italian fare.

Jerk Seasoning

Origin – Jamaica

Ingredients – Scotch bonnet pepper (or habanero), cinnamon, allspice, thyme, nutmeg, ginger, garlic, salt, scallion, brown sugar, soy, lime.

Flavor – Deeply flavorful blend that's spicy, herbaceous, acidic, nutty and salty.

Use on – Use with rice and beans or marinate grilled or roasted fruits and vegetables with before cooking. The tangy spice pairs well with naturally sweet foods like pineapple, mango, and sweet potatoes. Can be dried or in a sauce.

Old Bay

Origin – American Southeast

Ingredients – Celery seed, salt, paprika, red pepper, black pepper, other spices.

Flavor – Sweet, salty flavor with tang from a celery seed and a slight spice.

Used on – Versatile blend traditionally used on crab and other seafood. Can be sprinkled on fries, popcorn, corn on the cob, grilled veggies, pasta, veggie chowders and mock seafood dishes.

Quatre Episce

Origin – France

Ingredients – White (or black) pepper, ginger, nutmeg, clove.

Flavor – Warm and earthy blend that adds depth of flavor and complexity to dishes.

Use on – Often found in soups, stews, ragouts and other slowly-cooked dishes.

Za'atar

Origin – Middle East

Ingredients – Oregano, thyme, cumin, sesame seeds, salt, coriander, sumac, pepper flake.

Description – Woodsy, floral blend with a nutty finish from the sesame seeds.

Use it on – Salads, with grilled or roasted vegetables or to season hummus and other dips.

Section Six

Recipes

Recipe

1

Date _____

Prep time _____ Cook time _____ Serves _____

Ingredients

Directions

Notes

Recipe

Date

Prep time _____ Cook time _____ Serves _____

Ingredients

Directions

Notes

2

Recipe _____ Date _____

Prep time _____   Cook time _____   Serves _____

Ingredients

_____   _____
_____   _____
_____   _____
_____   _____
_____   _____
_____   _____

Directions

_____
_____
_____
_____
_____
_____
_____
_____
_____

Notes

_____

Recipe

Date

Prep time Cook time Serves

Ingredients

Directions

Notes

4

Recipe

5

Date _____

Prep time _____ Cook time _____ Serves _____

Ingredients

Directions

Notes

Recipe

Date

Prep time _____ Cook time _____ Serves _____

Ingredients

Directions

Notes

6

Recipe

Date

Prep time _____ Cook time _____ Serves _____

Ingredients

Directions

Notes

7

Recipe

Date

Prep time _____ Cook time _____ Serves _____

Ingredients

Directions

Notes

Recipe

Date

Prep time   Cook time   Serves

Ingredients

Directions

Notes

9

Recipe

Date

Prep time   Cook time   Serves

10

Ingredients

Directions

Notes

Recipe

Date

Prep time Cook time Serves

Ingredients

Directions

Notes

11

Recipe

Date

Prep time — **Cook time** — **Serves**

Ingredients

Directions

Notes

12

Recipe

Date

Prep time ___ Cook time ___ Serves ___

Ingredients

Directions

Notes

Recipe

14

Date _____

Prep time _____ Cook time _____ Serves _____

Ingredients

Directions

Notes

Recipe

15

Date _____

Prep time _____ Cook time _____ Serves _____

Ingredients

Directions

Notes

Recipe

16

Date _____

Prep time _____ Cook time _____ Serves _____

Ingredients

Directions

Notes

Recipe

17

Date _____

Prep time _____ Cook time _____ Serves _____

Ingredients

Directions

Notes

Recipe

Date

Prep time ———— Cook time ———— Serves ————

Ingredients

Directions

Notes

18

Recipe

19

Date

Prep time   Cook time   Serves

Ingredients

Directions

Notes

Recipe

Date _____ **20**

Prep time _____ Cook time _____ Serves _____

Ingredients

Directions

Notes

Recipe

Date

Prep time _____ Cook time _____ Serves _____

Ingredients

Directions

Notes

21

Recipe

Date

Prep time _____ Cook time _____ Serves _____

Ingredients

Directions

Notes

22

Recipe

Date

Prep time ___ Cook time ___ Serves ___

Ingredients

Directions

Notes

Recipe

24

Date _____

Prep time _____   Cook time _____   Serves _____

Ingredients

Directions

Notes

Recipe

25

Date _____

Prep time _____   Cook time _____   Serves _____

Ingredients

Directions

Notes

Recipe

Date

Prep time _____ Cook time _____ Serves _____

Ingredients

Directions

Notes

26

Recipe

27

Date _____

Prep time _____   Cook time _____   Serves _____

Ingredients

_____   _____
_____   _____
_____   _____
_____   _____
_____   _____
_____   _____

Directions

_____
_____
_____
_____
_____
_____
_____
_____
_____
_____

Notes

_____
_____

Recipe

28

Date

Prep time   Cook time   Serves

Ingredients

Directions

Notes

Recipe

29

Date

Prep time   Cook time   Serves

Ingredients

Directions

Notes

Recipe

30

Date _____

Prep time _____ Cook time _____ Serves _____

Ingredients

_____
_____
_____
_____
_____
_____

_____
_____
_____
_____
_____
_____

Directions

_____
_____
_____
_____
_____
_____
_____
_____
_____

Notes

_____

Recipe

31

Date

Prep time Cook time Serves

Ingredients

Directions

Notes

Recipe

32

Date

Prep time   Cook time   Serves

Ingredients

Directions

Notes

Recipe

Date

Prep time _____ Cook time _____ Serves _____

Ingredients

Directions

Notes

33

Recipe

Date

Prep time ———— Cook time ———— Serves ————

Ingredients

Directions

Notes

34

Recipe

Date

Prep time   Cook time   Serves

Ingredients

Directions

Notes

35

Recipe

36

Date

Prep time Cook time Serves

Ingredients

Directions

Notes

Recipe

Date

Prep time ___ Cook time ___ Serves ___

Ingredients

Directions

Notes

Recipe

38

Date _____

Prep time _____ Cook time _____ Serves _____

Ingredients

_____ _____
_____ _____
_____ _____
_____ _____
_____ _____

Directions

_____
_____
_____
_____
_____
_____
_____
_____

_____ Notes _____

_____

Recipe

Date

Prep time Cook time Serves

Ingredients

Directions

Notes

39

Recipe

Date _____

Prep time _____ Cook time _____ Serves _____

Ingredients

Directions

Notes

Recipe

Date

Prep time _____ Cook time _____ Serves _____

Ingredients

Directions

Notes

41

Recipe

Date

Prep time _____ Cook time _____ Serves _____

Ingredients

Directions

Notes

42

Recipe

43

Date

Prep time Cook time Serves

Ingredients

Directions

Notes

Recipe

Date

Prep time ———————— Cook time ———————— Serves ————

Ingredients

Directions

—— Notes ——

44

Recipe

Date

Prep time — Cook time — Serves

Ingredients

Directions

Notes

45

Recipe

46

Date _____

Prep time _____ Cook time _____ Serves _____

Ingredients

Directions

Notes

Recipe

47

Date

Prep time   Cook time   Serves

Ingredients

Directions

Notes

Recipe

48

Date

Prep time   Cook time   Serves

Ingredients

Directions

Notes

Recipe

49

Date _____

Prep time _____ Cook time _____ Serves _____

Ingredients

Directions

Notes

Recipe

50

Date

Prep time Cook time Serves

Ingredients

Directions

Notes

Recipe

51

Date _____

Prep time _____ Cook time _____ Serves _____

Ingredients

Directions

Notes

Recipe

52

Date _____

Prep time _____ Cook time _____ Serves _____

Ingredients

Directions

Notes

Recipe

Date

Prep time ____ Cook time ____ Serves ____

Ingredients

Directions

Notes

Recipe

54

Date _____

Prep time _____ Cook time _____ Serves _____

Ingredients

_____ _____
_____ _____
_____ _____
_____ _____
_____ _____
_____ _____

Directions

_____
_____
_____
_____
_____
_____
_____
_____
_____

_____ Notes _____

_____

Recipe

Date

Prep time ___ Cook time ___ Serves ___

Ingredients

Directions

Notes

Recipe

Date

Prep time ———— Cook time ———— Serves ————

Ingredients

Directions

Notes

56

Recipe

Date

Prep time ____ Cook time ____ Serves ____

Ingredients

Directions

Notes

57

Recipe

58

Date

Prep time   Cook time   Serves

Ingredients

Directions

Notes

Recipe

59

Date

Prep time   Cook time   Serves

Ingredients

Directions

Notes

Recipe

Date

Prep time ———————— Cook time ———————— Serves ————

Ingredients

Directions

— Notes —

60

Recipe

61

Date _____

Prep time _____ Cook time _____ Serves _____

Ingredients

Directions

Notes

Recipe

Date

Prep time Cook time Serves

Ingredients

Directions

Notes

62

Recipe

63

Date _____

Prep time _____ Cook time _____ Serves _____

Ingredients

Directions

Notes

Recipe

Date

Prep time — Cook time — Serves

Ingredients

Directions

Notes

64

Recipe

Date

Prep time   Cook time   Serves

65

Ingredients

Directions

Notes

Recipe

Date _____

Prep time _____ **Cook time** _____ **Serves** _____

Ingredients

Directions

Notes

Recipe

Date

Prep time _____ Cook time _____ Serves _____

Ingredients

Directions

Notes

Recipe

Date

Prep time — Cook time — Serves

Ingredients

Directions

Notes

68

Recipe

Date

Prep time Cook time Serves

Ingredients

Directions

Notes

69

… Recipe ……………………………… Date ………

Prep time ……………… Cook time ……………… Serves ………

Ingredients

Directions

— Notes —

Recipe

71

Date

Prep time   Cook time   Serves

Ingredients

Directions

Notes

Recipe

72

Date

Prep time   Cook time   Serves

Ingredients

Directions

Notes

Recipe

73

Date _____

Prep time _____ Cook time _____ Serves _____

Ingredients

Directions

Notes

Recipe

Date

Prep time ___ Cook time ___ Serves ___

Ingredients

Directions

Notes

Recipe

75

Date _____

Prep time _____ Cook time _____ Serves _____

Ingredients

Directions

Notes

Recipe

76

Date _____

Prep time _____ Cook time _____ Serves _____

Ingredients

Directions

Notes

Recipe

Date

Prep time ___ Cook time ___ Serves ___

Ingredients

Directions

Notes

Recipe

Date

Prep time _____ Cook time _____ Serves _____

Ingredients

Directions

Notes

78

Recipe

Date

Prep time _____ Cook time _____ Serves _____

Ingredients

Directions

Notes

79

Recipe

Prep time _____ Cook time _____ Serves _____ Date _____

80

Ingredients

Directions

Notes

Recipe

Date _____

81

Prep time _____ Cook time _____ Serves _____

Ingredients

Directions

Notes

Recipe

Date

Prep time   Cook time   Serves

Ingredients

Directions

Notes

82

Recipe

Date

Prep time Cook time Serves

Ingredients

Directions

Notes

83

Recipe

84

Date

Prep time Cook time Serves

Ingredients

Directions

Notes

Recipe

85

Date _____

Prep time _____   Cook time _____   Serves _____

Ingredients

Directions

Notes

Recipe

Date

Prep time _____ Cook time _____ Serves _____

Ingredients

Directions

Notes

86

Recipe

Date

Prep time _____ Cook time _____ Serves _____

Ingredients

Directions

Notes

87

Recipe

Date

Prep time   Cook time   Serves

Ingredients

Directions

Notes

88

Recipe

Date

Prep time _____ Cook time _____ Serves _____

Ingredients

Directions

Notes

89

Recipe

90

Date _____

Prep time _____ Cook time _____ Serves _____

Ingredients

Directions

Notes

Recipe

Date

Prep time ___ Cook time ___ Serves ___

Ingredients

Directions

Notes

91

Recipe

Date

Prep time _____ Cook time _____ Serves _____

Ingredients

Directions

Notes

92

Recipe

Date

Prep time — Cook time — Serves

Ingredients

Directions

Notes

Recipe

Date

Prep time   Cook time   Serves

Ingredients

Directions

Notes

94

Recipe

Date

Prep time ____ Cook time ____ Serves ____

Ingredients

Directions

Notes

Recipe

96

Date

Prep time Cook time Serves

Ingredients

Directions

Notes

Recipe

97

Date

Prep time   Cook time   Serves

Ingredients

Directions

Notes

Recipe

Date

Prep time _____ Cook time _____ Serves _____

Ingredients

Directions

Notes

Recipe

99

Date

Prep time   Cook time   Serves

Ingredients

Directions

Notes

Recipe

100

Date _____

Prep time _____ Cook time _____ Serves _____

Ingredients

Directions

Notes

www.ingramcontent.com/pod-product-compliance
Lightning Source LLC
Chambersburg PA
CBHW081709100526
44590CB00022B/3716